# TURNING BACK TIME ON

# *Abbeydale Road*

Published by **Arc Publishing and Print**
166 Knowle Lane, Bents Green, Sheffield S11 9SJ.
t: 07809 172872  w: www.sheffieldbooks.co.uk
e: chris@arcbooks.co.uk

# Acknowledgements

Many thanks to the following people who supplied photographs and information for this book.

Special thanks to the staff at Sheffield Central Library, Local Studies Department for permission to reproduce photographs from their collection.
Thanks to Sheffield Newspapers for the use of their archive photos.
Many thanks to Geoff Bannister who I tried very hard to get in contact with, but to no avail.
Joyce Parker for her cartoon on page 35.
David Bradley for his photos of the Beauchief area.
Chris Hobbs for Abbeydale Grange information.
To Beauchief Abbey for the history of the Abbey.
Brenda Keeling for her help writing the book.

Text copyright 2011 © Chris Keeling

The rights of Chris Keeling and his work has been asserted by him in accordance with the
Copyright, Design Patent Act 1988

November 2011

ISBN: 978-1-906722-21-0

Published by Arc Publishing and Print
166 Knowle Lane
Sheffield
S11 9SJ

Telephone 07809 172872
Email: chris@arcbooks.co.uk

This book is dedicated to the late
**William Joseph Grenville Massey**
Former Head Master of Abbeydale Grange Comprehensive School

# Introduction

Abbeydale Road and Abbeydale Road South leads south-west from the suburb of Highfield to the railway bridge over the Dore and Chinley railway, before becoming Baslow Road. The road begins at the junction with London Road near the former Royal Hotel public house and this book follows its history along its four mile route. It passes through several districts which are all part of the Abbey Dale or Valley. One of these areas is Beauchief and its Abbey after which Abbeydale is named.

The River Sheaf flows through the dale and you will see the industries that have grown up beside it. You will also find parks, woods, halls, schools, churches, past railway stations and many other places of interest.

Of course, the road has changed over the years - but not drastically. The horse drawn traffic has gone along with the trams - but it is still a very pleasant road with some lovely buildings and open spaces leading out to the Baslow Road and the beautiful Derbyshire countryside beyond.

I hope you enjoy the journey.

# Index

# The Start at Highfields

1. Highfield Branch Library

2. Trinity Methodist Church

3. John Dennell, Dentist Surgery

4. Herschell Road

5. Wolseley Road

6. Sheffield & Ecclesall Co-op

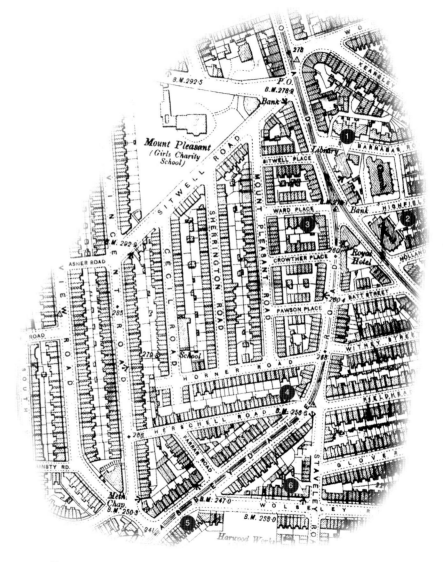

Map date 1905

Trinity Methodist Church, Highfield taken from the junction of Abbeydale Road & London Road showing Highfield Place on the left. The church was founded in the Methodist Tradition; being built over 100 years ago, it has a long history of adapting to the needs of the local community. Some years ago it merged with St. Barnabas Church opposite (now a sheltered complex) and more recently it has welcomed partner churches from the Apostolic and African traditions who also worship in the church.

c1910 photo of Highfield Branch Library on London Road just before the junction with Abbeydale Road. This library was a welcome addition to the area and was widely used especially on a Saturday by both adults and children.

This photo was taken in the summer of 1939 and looks down London Road, Highfield Library is on the right. From this point you could travel by tram to Millhouses using two routes - Woodseats via Millhouses or Millhouses via Woodseats. The second route took much longer - travelling along Abbey Lane, passing Beauchief Abbey and along Abbeydale Road South to Millhouses.

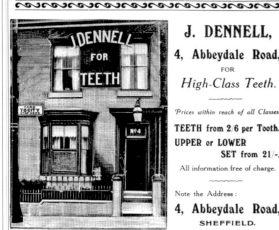

J. DENNELL,

4, Abbeydale Road,

FOR

*High-Class Teeth.*

*Prices within reach of all Classes.*

TEETH from 2/6 per Tooth.
UPPER or LOWER
SET from 21/-.

All information free of charge.

Note the Address :

4, Abbeydale Road,
SHEFFIELD.

Telephone 33 Sharrow.

The beginning of Abbeydale Road at the junction with London Road in 1923. The dentists belonging to John Dennell is at number 4 Abbeydale Road. You can see the lamp outside, which is also in the advert opposite.

Evening rush hour at the start of Abbeydale Road where a parked lorry outside the Royal Hotel prevents a bus pulling into the kerb. Parked lorries often caused hold ups at Highfields junction creating a queue of vehicles on London Road. Nothing changes,  Lorries still pull up wherever they want - even with double yellow lines!

Both these pictures were taken in July 1961. This one was taken from the junction with Herschell Road. Premises on the right include numbers 76 to 86 which was B.J. Williams & Son Ltd, Motor Engineers and number 94 which was Richard's Furniture Brokers.

Abbeydale Road at junction of Wolseley Road.

No. 1 Branch of Sheffield & Ecclesall Co-op, at number 24-32 Wolseley Road just off Abbeydale Road. The number of branches increased rapidly during the 20's and 30's. The one at Beauchief was number 36.

A recent photo from 2001 shows the Second Church of Christ Scientists & Reading Room taken from Abbeydale Road looking towards South View Road & Vincent Road. The church was originally Abbeydale Primitive Church which opened in 1891.

# Chippinghouse Road to Sheldon Road

**7** 164 -152, Abbeydale Road

**8** Chippinghouse Road

**9** Abbeydale Congregational church

**10** J. Gilbert Jackson's Chemist

**11** St. Peter's Church

**12** Abbeydale Picture House

**13** Sheldon Road

Map date 1905

11

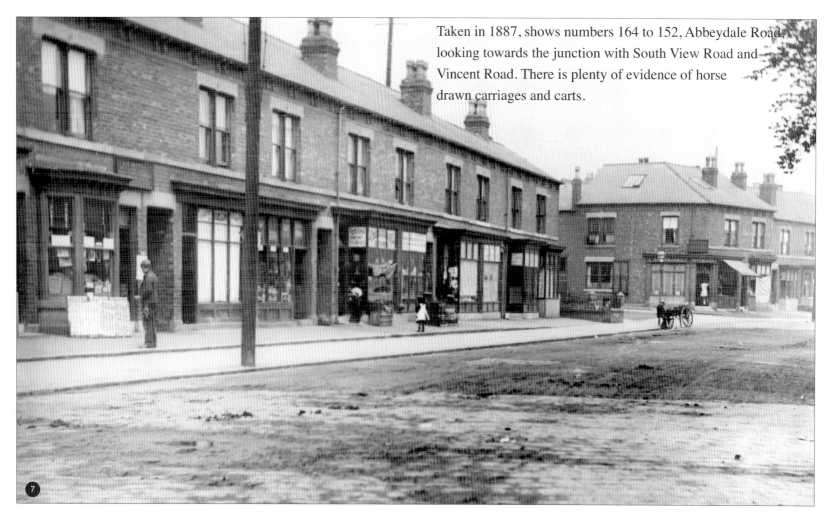

Taken in 1887, shows numbers 164 to 152, Abbeydale Road, looking towards the junction with South View Road and Vincent Road. There is plenty of evidence of horse drawn carriages and carts.

7

A great photo from October 1965 shows a rather out dated pram being pushed across the road. Chippinghouse Road is on the right with the old Post Office on the corner. On looking even closer you can see Green Brothers (Dore) Ltd sign written on the van. They continued trading until approx 2005.

c1900. Thankfully the night soil cart in the centre of the picture disappeared long ago. Sanitation as we know it today was a relatively modern thing. In many roads, sewers were not laid to all of the houses until well into the 1920's. Abbeydale Congregational Church is in the background.

J. Gilbert Jackson's Chemist at numbers 338 & 340 Abbeydale Road. Note the very ornamental lamp outside the shop.

The Mother of God Roman Catholic Church, This church was Abbeydale Congregational church in 1903, with its associated Sunday School.

Inside J. Gilbert Jackson's Chemist shop.

When St Peter's church was demolished in 2003, talks began with St Oswald's about the two parishes joining together as a single community. This happened in 2004 when the two congregations began worshipping together as one. In July 2009 the separate parishes of St Peter's Abbeydale and St Oswald's Millhouses became the one parish of St Peter and St Oswald Sheffield.

The demolition of St. Peter's Church, Machon Bank & Empire Road in 2003, taken from the opposite side of Abbeydale Road.

St. Peter's Church, Machon Bank in 1993 at the junction of Empire Road looking towards the Abbeydale Picture House.

15

Abbeydale Picture House was designed by Dixon & Stienley and opened on the 20th December 1920. It was taken over by the Star Group in the 1950s and closed on the 5th July 1975.

Abbeydale Picture House (later Abbeydale Cinema) was opened by the Lord Mayor of Sheffield on the 20th December 1920. The picture house was the largest and most luxurious cinema in Sheffield and was often called Picture Palace because it was decorated in cream and gold with green velvet seats made of dark mahogany. It had many intricate decorations and carvings as well as a mosaic floor in the foyer and a glass canopy with a marble pillar on the outside of the building. The first film shown was The Call of the Road. The cinema had seating for 1,560 people and also included a ballroom and a billiard hall. Cine-variety played a major role at the Abbeydale until 1930 when the "talkies" talking films came in and the stage was then used purely to house the sound equipment. In the mid-1950s the cinema was taken over by the Star Cinema Group which meant the entire building was redecorated and new cinema technology fitted including a new permanent wide screen. The cinema closed on the 5th July 1975 and was used as an office furniture showroom. In 1989 the building was given a Grade II listing by English Heritage. In 1991 the sprung floor in the ballroom was ripped out and Abbey Snooker and Bar Abbey moved in. In 2003 the Friends of Abbeydale Picture House—boasting patrons including Michael Palin, Peter Stringfellow and the John Lewis Partnership—was formed to "restore and manage the 'Picture Palace' as a community centre for the performing arts and visual media." They officially became the owners of the building on the 21st December 2005. The Abbeydale Picture House has regular performances and fundraisers to try and raise money towards its restoration.

This early photo of Arthur East's Premises at 447 Abbeydale Road was taken around 1910, before the Picture House was built. It was attached to the left hand side of Arthur's house in 1920.

This aerial View was taken in 1935. In the centre is the picture palace. The terraced houses to the right have all gone to make way for shops and a play ground.

Tavistock Rd, Empire Rd, St. Peter's Church & Machon Bank can be seen in the foreground. Little London Works, Broadfield Rd and the River Sheaf are in the background.

The stretch of road near the historic Abbeydale Picture House is still known as the 'Antiques Quarter'. Many of the junk shops have now gone but it was very enjoyable to root around in what were simply houses accommodating floor to ceiling goods.

Elizabeth Fox pictured here outside her home, lived at Sheldon Lodge for over 30 years. It was demolished in the early 1900's

c1910 picture of the bottom of Sheldon Road. You can see numbers 444 to 448 Abbeydale Road & numbers 86 & 88 Sheldon Road. These properties were bought by the Yorkshire Penny Bank.

# Broadfield to Woodseats Road

**14** Broadfield Road

**15** Broadfield Hotel

**16** Abbeydale Board School

**17** Tom Bond's Grocery Shop

**18** Gatefield House

**19** Mary Somerfield Family Butcher

**20** Junction of Woodseats Road

Map date 1905

Tram 199 heading along Abbeydale Road towards Millhouses. The corner of Broadfield Road can be seen between the bus and tram. Broadfield Road was originally called Rufford Road. (See map on previous page)

The Broadfield Hotel with landlord
Albert Twigg is standing in the doorway.
Abbeydale Board School is in
the background.

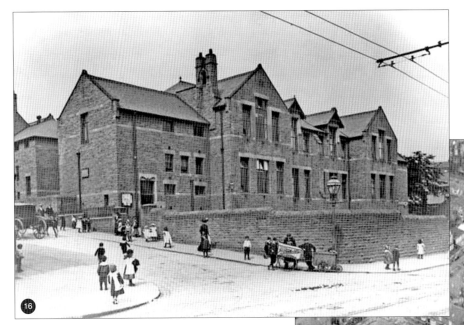

An aerial view of Abbeydale Nursery, First and Middle School, taken in February 1996. Prominent roads include Glen Road, Gatefield Road, Grove Road and Sheldon Road.

Abbeydale Board School so named when it was opened in 1890 by John Daniel Leader, an author of several books on Sheffield history. The school is now called Abbeydale Primary School.

23

An artists impression by W. Topham of Broadfield toll bar or sometimes called Abbeydale Road toll bar. The gate would have been near the bottom of Sheldon Road. It was closed 1873.

A similar view taken in the rush hour during the recent winter of 2010.

A 1963 photo looking out of town towards the junction with Leyburn Road on the left. The premises of Albt. E. Butterworth the cycle dealer are on the corner and still trading today. You might be able to make out the penny farthing cycle that used to be on display above the window.

October 1989 sees Abbeydale Road under a few feet of water. This was not due to heavy rain fall that can cause flooding on this stretch of road but to a burst water main. The shops and houses between Marden Road and Gatefield Road were worst hit.

A well known owner of this house was Thomas Bagshaw Cockayne the co-founder of the department store T.B.&W. Cockayne which stood at the top of Angel Street. The store was badly damaged in the Second World War. In the 30's the house became the Gatefield House Social Club.

Ada Bond outside Tom Bond's Grocery
Shop at number 605 Abbeydale Road.
The photo was taken around 1933.

A newspaper advert from 1905 for Mary
Somerfield Family Butcher at 725 Abbeydale
Road. It was on the corner of Langdale Road
and is now a sandwich shop.

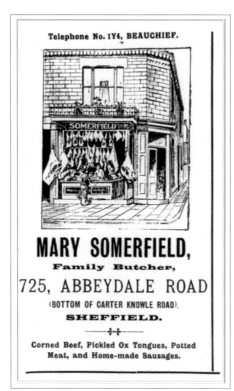

Telephone No. 1Y4, BEAUCHIEF.

**MARY SOMERFIELD,**
**Family Butcher,**
725, **ABBEYDALE ROAD**
(BOTTOM OF CARTER KNOWLE ROAD).
**SHEFFIELD.**

Corned Beef, Pickled Ox Tongues, Potted
Meat, and Home-made Sausages.

This 1924 photo of Mr. Walter Mitchell
and his lorry which was used by T.E.
Swan a grocer on Abbeydale Road.

Sixty years separate these two photographs. The road on the right (shown in the earliest picture) is Langdale Road, one of a group of roads named after places in the Lake District.

In many ways the pictures are very recognisable - the buildings, the pavement and wooded area. But, the gas lamps have gone. So have the open topped tram and tram lines. Cars have taken over from the horse - drawn vehicles and we no longer see many bowler hats.

27

c1918. Many houses between Grasmere Road and Windermere Road have recently been converted into shops. Shentall's on the corner was a well known shop in the area. When the Co-op opened across the road, Shentall's lost a lot of trade and closed soon after.

On the right of this recent photo you can see Rawson's Bathroom Showroom. This building started out as a Co-op. Barmouth Road is on the left with Woodseats Road on the right.

# Abbeydale House to Hastings Road

21 Abbeydale House

22 St Oswald's Church

23 Holt House

24 Abbeydale Grange

25 Millhouses Hotel

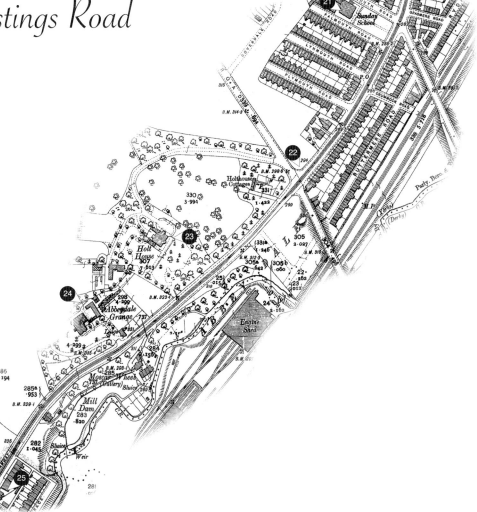

Map date 1905

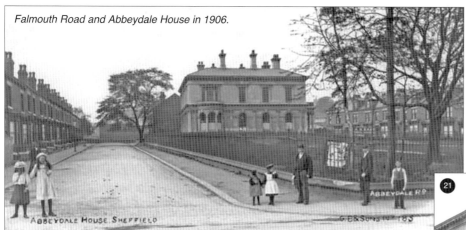

*Falmouth Road and Abbeydale House in 1906.*

Abbeydale House which still stands hidden behind Eric Gilbert's carpet showroom was once described as a "First class mansion with pleasure grounds commanding beautiful views over the surrounding county, which is richly wooded and highly picturesque". At least that's what it said in the auction notice in 1860 when the house was advertised for sale. This followed the death of John Rodgers, head of the world famous cutlery firm Joseph Rodgers and Sons for whom the house was built in 1850.

The building was taken over by Snowite laundry. This rather poor photo shows the fleet of Morris Oxford vans lined up on Barmouth Road. The now listed large chimney behind the house is still there today.

*Abbeydale house as it is today.*

Whoever gave planning permission to attach a red brick monstrosity to the front of Abbeydale house needs locking up.

A 1935 aerial view from Woodseats Road with Abbeydale House and its grounds in the top left to Bannerdale Road and Archer Road with the grounds of Holt House on the right.

Some houses on Bannerdale Road had Coach Houses built at the end of their gardens. There was living accommodation above the stables for the coachman.

Abbeydale Road in 1906

A photo taken in 1920 of a Whit Sunday walking group on Buttermere Road. (Most probably from St. Oswald's Church)

Some people will remember the Saturday night dances at St. Oswalds Church Hall. They were very popular for many years - starting, I believe, in the 1940's.

Holt House and Grange House were the two mansions that formed part of the of the all girls high school - Grange Grammar School that lay adjacent to the Boys Grammar School on Abbeydale Road, Millhouses. In 1806 Holt House was owned by Joseph Wilson Esq. and in 1834 by a John Rodgers. John was a leading member of the firm of Joseph Rodgers, who was living in Abbeydale House when he died at the age of 80, in 1859 (He is buried in Ecclesall Churchyard). The 1861 Directory states that the occupant was Robert Newbold, merchant and manufacturer . Hunter's Hallamshire states that "In Abbeydale there is a chaste mansion erected by the late John Rodgers for his own habitation. It is now the property of his nephew who occupies it". It appears that John Rodgers erected Abbeydale Grange whilst he was living at Holt House and then moved into it. The 1869 edition of Hunter's Hallamshire then goes on to remark that Holt House was recently rebuilt on the same site by its new owner John Firth, merchant and manufacturer who was connected to the famous Sheffield steelmaking company.

In 1918 Holt House was bought from the Firth family by Sheffield Education Committee to house Abbeydale Girls Secondary School later to become Abbeydale Grammar School. The School was housed here until the new school was built in 1939. The Grange then became part of Hurlfield Girls Grammar School sharing a building with the Arbourthorne Central Junior School. As its numbers grew it took over the Grange, Holt House and a wooden hall. In 1947 additional prefabricated buildings were added to the Holt House estate and the whole of Hurfield Grammar School was amalgamated on the site. The gym and the assembly hall were added five years later in 1952. In September 1954 the school's name was changed to Grange Grammar School and it

Holt House, c1900.

remained that way until it joined Abbeydale Boys Grammar School and Abbeydale Girls Grammar School to become Abbeydale Grange.

All that remains now is the boarded up lodge,
situated opposite Tesco Petrol Station.

A 1963 photo of Grange Grammar School for Girls.
During the 1940's when Hurlfield Grammar School was housed here - no
teachers had cars and this area in front of the school was used for playing rounders.
The music room to the left of the picture had lovely views over the grounds.

Holt House, unfortunately in a derelict state after being vandalised and set
on fire some years ago. Now demolished, an estate of new private houses
has been built on the extensive and once beautiful grounds.

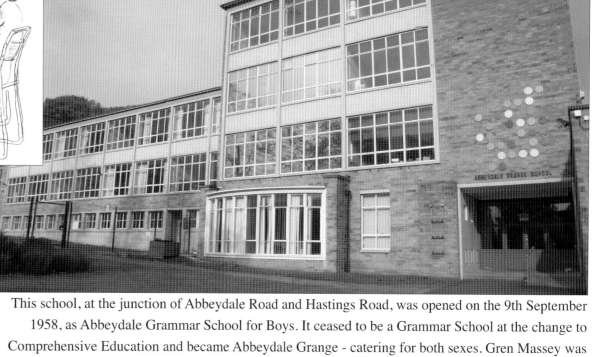

A cartoon drawing by an unknown artist, possibly a pupil at the school.

It shows Gren Massey - Head Teacher making a speech.

Joe Fielding - Head of 6th Form, who looks asleep.

Norman Jepson - Deputy Head, making notes and Irene Gordon, also Deputy Head, listening carefully or possibly wishing he would sit down..

This school, at the junction of Abbeydale Road and Hastings Road, was opened on the 9th September 1958, as Abbeydale Grammar School for Boys. It ceased to be a Grammar School at the change to Comprehensive Education and became Abbeydale Grange - catering for both sexes. Gren Massey was Headmaster of the boys grammar School between 1962 and 1969. He continued as Headmaster of the new Abbeydale Grange Comprehensive from 1969 - 1982.

Two aerial views from 1994 with Abbeydale Road travelling through Millhouses and the surrounding area.

In the centre is Abbeydale Grange Schools. Right is Archer Road and what remains of Laycocks Engineering can be seen in the foreground. The start of Millhouses Park is on the left.

Millhouses Hotel number 251 Abbeydale Road. The hotel is still very recognisable today. Part of the building to the right of the picture was knocked down many years ago to make room for a car park. c1900.

This line of terrace houses are known as Moscar Villas. c1910

37

# Abbeydale Road South - Millhouses

26   E.H. Middleton & Son (Decorators)

27   Junction of Archer Road

28   Millhouses Corn Mill

29   Robin Hood Hotel

30   Millhouses & Ecclesall Station

31   Waggon and Horses Public House

32   Millhouses Tram Terminus

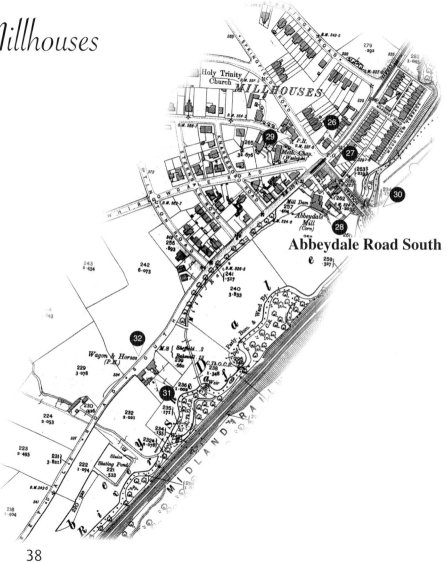

**Abbeydale Road South**

Map date 1905

38

This photograph was taken on the 12th December 1940, after one of Hitlers bombs had destroyed the property on the left and severely damaged the shop next door. Another bomb landed across the road and hit the end terrace house at the junction of Archer road. That property was rebuilt and is now an HSBC Bank.

This later shot from 1962 has E.H. Middleton occupying the shop on the front, which is now a fish and chip shop. R. Handley, Greengrocer can be seen next door. Middletons are still in business. operating from the rear of the building.

c1910. Tram 217 approaching Millhouses Tram Terminus.

Abbeydale Road meets Abbeydale Road South in 1899. Shops from left to right are Hay & Son, Wine Merchant at number 991, Millhouses Post Office at number 993, Confectioners at number 995 and Drapers Grocers at number 999.

Abbeydale Road at the junction of Archer Road in 1952. A branch of the National Provincial Bank is on the corner.

41

Millhouses Corn Mill, off Abbeydale Road South, 22nd June 1893. Parts of the old corn mill from which Millhouses gets its name, can still be seen today, but the old mill dam was filled in long ago. It was mentioned in a 13th century document.

A derelict part of Millhouses Corn Mill at number 9 Abbeydale Road South. This picture is from 1950. Soon afterwards the building was pulled down.

A busy day at the bottom of Whirlowdale Road in the 1920's.

The shop pictured on the corner was a Chemists for many years, (1920's to 2005 approx) in the 1920's and 30's it served a large area - Millhouses, Beauchief and as far as Whirlow. The gentleman who owned it, prior to the Second World War, was very popular - especially with the young mothers of the area. He would weigh their babies and give advice on health and feeding, which was invaluable in those days. He was, however, of German origin and in 1939 he was sent to live on the Isle of Man for the duration of the war. He was sadly missed.

The Robin Hood Hotel at the junction of Springfield Road (right) and Millhouses Lane (left). This photograph was taken in 1942 from the corner of Whirlowdale Road and Abbeydale Road South.

c1920. Millhouses Wesleyan Methodist Chapel is in background. This photo is taken before the extension was built to the front, which can be seen on the previous page.

A very early picture of the Robin Hood Hotel when it was a small country pub. It has been extended to the rear but thankfully has retained its recognisable frontage.

General View of Millhouses taken c1930. Millhouses & Ecclesall Station and the Station House can be seen to the right. **30**

Millhouses and Ecclesall Station.

Surprisingly many suburban railway stations had porters to help passengers with their luggage.

When the station opened in 1870 it was called Ecclesall, but this was changed, first to Ecclesall & Millhouses and later Mill Houses & Ecclesall before becoming Millhouses and Ecclesall. It was situated on the Midland Main Line between Heeley railway station and Beauchief station, and was accessed from the Archer Road overbridge, near the junction of Abbeydale Road and Millhouses Lane. The station closed on June 10th 1968, and remained derelict for many years. The station buildings and platforms were finally removed in the 1980s, but the stationmaster's house survives as a private home.

Waggon and Horses and outbuildings (later converted into garages). c1860

c1890. Waggon & Horses - still not much has been developed around about.

Very early photo of the Waggon and Horses, when the surrounding area was farm land.

c1950 Waggon and Horses and former outbuildings are now converted into a garage. Much busier now as the trams have arrived.

As it is now, with people enjoying a drink in the sunshine.

Millhouses Tram Terminus.

The Millhouses tram turned round the loop and made its way back to the centre of Sheffield whilst other trams went on to Beauchief and along Abbey Lane to Woodseats. There was one nasty accident at the beginning of this loop when two trams collided. The points on the line had not been changed.

Works car 330 is seen here at Millhouses. The abandoned loop in the background is in the process of being resurfaced for buses.

A nice sunny day at Millhouses. Many families used the trams to get to the very popular Millhouses Park. The Laycock Engineering Company can be seen in the background beyond the railway station bridge.

# Millhouses Park to Abbey Lane - Beauchief Corner

**33** Millhouses Lido

**34** Beauchief Hotel

**35** Beauchief Post Office

**36** Beauchief and Abbey Dale Station

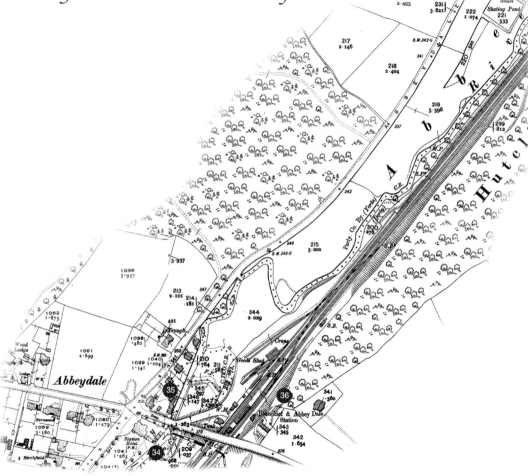

Map date 1905

Millhouses Lido in its hay day. Great times when health and safety rules were never an issue. By the 1960s the park could attract up to 50,000 visitors on summer weekends. In the 1980s, the lido was closed.

This photograph was taken in 1958. The River Sheaf ran through these pools that were painted blue. They were enjoyed by many local children. Finally in the 1990's they were closed due to concern over the pollution in the river.

Sheffield Spartan Swimmers - Millhouses Pool 1933-4.
The swimmers tradition would be to break the ice ever year and swim a few lengths. A few of this group seem more interested in eating it.

The boating pond has been re-opened with the original boats. The cafe has had a new lease of life and is now run by a group calling themselves the Pudding Ladies.

The water was really rather murky - you certainly couldn't see the bottom of the pool. But it was a very large pool and most attractive on a hot summers day.

This selection of photographs were taken on the 12th September 1960 by Geoff Bannister, a couple of weeks before the last tram ran along this line.

They show the stretch of road between Millhouses Park and Beauchief Corner. As soon as the trams stopped running work started on changing the road into a duel carriageway.

This is one of the specially painted trams used in the last week of Sheffield Trams. Civic dignitaries rode the last tram into the city centre from Beauchief on a wet Saturday night where they had dinner at the Town Hall.

Abbeydale Station Hotel. c1918.

This photo shows a busy Bank Holiday with lots of people travelling along the road. Many are picking up or dropping off at the station which is just out of view on Abbey Lane.

The renamed Beauchief Hotel in October 1979. You can just make out the filling station in the background. This replaced the Post Office that was there for many years.

The Beauchief Hotel as it is today with Christan's Restaurant.

Abbeydale Road South and the Abbey Lane junction in June 1964. The corner has changed completely since this photo. The old Beauchief Post Office in the centre has gone and was replaced by a filling station built further back to allow better visibility to traffic turning up Abbey Lane. This has also gone and a complex of apartments now sits on the site. The van is turning right onto Abbeydale Road South from Abbey Lane - this is still difficult today. One day a bright spark at the Highways Department might put a filter on these lights!

The house on the far left in this recent picture is the only recognisable building still standing.

I can't see any traffic lights at all in this photo from 1959. Note the sign to the R.A.F. Base - which was at Norton.

Beauchief and Abbey Dale Station, pre 1903. Local residents used the train to reach the beautiful Derbyshire countryside. Many also used them daily to get to their work in the city.

Beauchief and Abbey Dale Station, around 1908. Note the sign and the separate words for Abbey Dale. The Abbey Lane and Abbeydale Road South junction can be seen in the background along with Abbeydale Station Hotel. Modern houses now occupy the land between the station and the back of Abbeydale Road South.

Pictured on Abbeydale Road South, at the junction with Abbey Lane. The stone building to the left of the tram is Beauchief Hotel. Abbey Lane comes down between the Hotel and stone building to the left of the picture. Note the clock suspended on the lamp post, and the shelter at the tram stop to the right. After the Abbey Lane section to Woodseats closed on 1st March 1959 this was the terminus - the trailing points can be seen in the foreground, and the second set of tracks are covered with a crude layer of tarmac. This is now just an ordinary bus stop, and the road has been widened to take in the point where the tram is stopped. Car 502 is seen ready to depart for Vulcan Road on the morning of the last day of operation, torrential rain began at noon and did not cease until early evening. Vulcan Road was on the opposite side of the city, in the heart of industrial area.

Tram Car 222 seen arriving at
Beauchief Corner in the late fifties.

The murder of St. Thomas a Becket in Canterbury Cathedral on 29th December 1170 AD brought about the founding of the Abbey.

Robert Fitzranulph, Lord of Alfreton, was said to have felt remorse at Thomas a Becket's murder and gave land, sealing a charter granting the establishment of an Abbey at Beauchief which would be dedicated to "God, St Mary, St Thomas and the blessed brethren of Premontre"

A group of Premonstratensian white canons, an order founded by St Norbert at Premontre in France, settled at Beauchief and began building and establishing the Abbey. According to the records, the official founding day was 21st December 1183.

In the following years the Abbey was granted further land so that by 1300 possessions included land in Ecclesall, Fulwood, Chesterfield, Eckington, Staveley, Totley, Greenhill, Dore, Handley, Watchill and Dronfield. Records of the lands held by the Abbey and the life of the church were copied by the canons into a book known as the "Cartulary". This book is in its original bindings and held by the Archives of Sheffield City Council.

Henry VIII's and his Dissolution of the Monasteries saw an end to medieval church life at the Abbey.

On 4th February 1536 the Abbot of Beauchief, John Greenwood, handed over the Abbey keys to the King's representatives who smashed windows, stripped the lead from the roof and left the building to fall into ruin.

Following the enforced abandonment of the Abbey the King sold the land at Beauchief to Sir Nicholas Strelley for £223. In 1648 the land came by marriage, into the possession of the Pegge family.

By the 1660s the fabric of the Abbey had fallen into disrepair and much of the stone was used for the building of Beauchief Hall, a little further up the hill.

The Abbey Church building was restored in the 1660's by constructing a chapel that extended from the remains of the medieval Abbey tower. This chapel and tower remain as the church building today.

The Pegge family continued to own Beauchief Hall and the Abbey until 1923, when it passed to Mr. Frank Crawshaw and in 1931 he sold the land occupied today by Beauchief Golf Course to the Sheffield Corporation.

At the same time Mr. Crawshaw offered the Abbey, adjacent cottages, graveyard and Abbey grounds as a gift to the Corporation, for the Citizens of Sheffield, on condition that Church of England services should continue in the Abbey and that it should not be used for any other purpose.

*Beauchief Abbey. Not on Abbeydale Road I know, but very close and of cause the reason for many of the road names in the area, including Abbeydale Road.*

# Abbeydale Works to Twentywell Lane - Dore

**37** Abbeydale Works. (Abbeydale Industrial Hamlet)

**38** Beauchief Gardens

**39** Abbeydale Miniature Railway

**40** Licensed Victuallers Association Almshouses

**41** Dore and Totley Station

Map date 1905

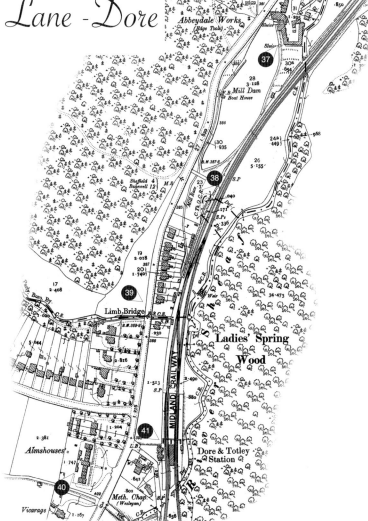

Abbeydale Industrial Hamlet is a unique eighteenth century industrial works. Originally called Abbeydale Works, it was one of the largest water-powered sites on the River Sheaf. The main products of the works were agricultural scythes, but other edge tools were made too, such as grass hooks and hay knives.

The site was used for iron forging for 500 years, although there is evidence of other metal working prior to 1200 AD. Its early history is intimately tied with the nearby Beauchief Abbey, which operated a smithy (blacksmith's shop) in the vicinity as well as number of mills along the River Sheaf.

The "Abbey Dale Works" as such, the buildings of which now form the Abbeydale Industrial Hamlet, are first formally recorded in 1714. From the 17th century onwards, the site primarily operated as a scythe works until, in 1933, it was closed by Tyzak Sons and Turner (tenants since 1849). In 1935 it was bought by the Alderman J. G. Graves Trust, which donated the site to the city. The works was briefly reopened during the Second World War to aid in Britain's war effort. It is now open to the public and many groups of school children enjoy educational tours of the hamlet. There is a cafe and book shop on site.

George Yardley's grave is a well known feature of Ecclesall Woods. The story goes that George, a charcoal burner who worked in the woods, burned to death in his cabin after a night out at the nearby Rising Sun on Abbey Lane.

Sampson Brookshaw the innkeeper and others had the memorial erected in his memory. He must have been a very good customer!

The memorial is dated 11th October 1786, but there are records of Ecclesall Woods dating as far back as 1319. Surprisingly the woods have only been open to the public since 1928.

Beauchief Gardens. The gardens were donated to the city by the J. G. Graves Trust in 1935, following the donation two years earlier of Abbeydale Industrial Hamlet immediately

*The old Beauchief Gardens sign which is no longer there.*

downstream. The gardens had always been well kept and possessed their own gardener. The level of care had declined until the 1990s when the Friends of Millhouses Park accepted the challenge of restoring the gardens. Clean-up events were organised in November 2004 and March 2005 to bring back the gardens to an acceptable level, a state which has been maintained.

Abbeydale miniature railway is tucked away on the edge of Ecclesall woods.

The miniature railway has been located at Abbeydale since 1978 and continues to attract sizable crowds when it opens to the public on various Sundays and Bank Holidays throughout the year. It is run by the local model engineering society, which is itself over 100 years old.

There are usually several trains available to ride, including a steam engine.

A love of trains and engineering seems to be the main motivation for the people involved and this helps to give the place a certain charm. The volunteers' enthusiasm is infectious and at a charge of 80p per person per ride it is obvious that they aren't in it for the money. In fact, any profit made is reinvested in the site.

In years to come I hope that the miniature railway is still around, providing a cheap afternoon out for many future generations.

In 1932, road signs were fixed on all first class roads that entered Sheffield. A very quiet day on Abbeydale Road South, maybe its because it looks rather wet and miserable. The track to the left is where the miniature railway is now.

40

Licensed Victuallers Association Almshouses, opposite Dore and Totley Station.

This very elaborate monument with its arches and spire, looks like a miniature model of a church. The monument was erected in memory of Alderman Thomas Wiley who raised funds and donated money for the building of the original Grimesthorpe Asylum in the 1850's. The monument was moved to its new home in front of the Almshouses when they were built in 1879.

Sheffield and Rotherham Licensed Victuallers Association. The almshouses were originally erected in Grimesthorpe in 1853 and moved to this location in 1879, when the surrounding fields in Grimesthorpe were being developed for industry, thus making living conditions difficult for the residents.

The Association purchased five and a half acres of land and two existing houses on this site for the cost of £6,000. The almshouses cost another £6,000 to build in 1878 and consist of twelve houses a library and a central hall for association meetings. The almshouses were used as a Red Cross Hospital during the First World War.

Dore and Totley Station opened on February 1st 1872 (at a building cost of £1517 and £450 for 2 acres of land) on the then two year-old Midland Main Line extension from Chesterfield to Sheffield. It was initially served by the local services on this line but later it was increased to six or seven weekday trains and three on Sundays.

In 1894 the station became the junction for the new Dore and Chinley line (now the Hope Valley Line). Dore & Totley Station Junction was at the south end of the station and the signal box stood in the angle between the Chesterfield and Chinley lines.

On October 9th 1907, a Sheffield to Birmingham and Bristol express train ran foul of the points at the station. One of the locomotives hit the platform and overturned. The driver and the second man were thrown from the cab but survived, and the passenger coaches fortunately stayed upright with no passengers injured. The station was closed to main line traffic and become an unstaffed halt in 1969.

Plans are being drawn up to double the size of the station by 2014. A additional platform, new footbridge, and 100 space car-park are to be provided.

'Railway Jim'.
James Henry Dyson, porter at Dore & Totley Station for 44 years.

# St John's Church to Baslow Road - Totley Rise

**42** St John's Church

**43** Abbeydale Tennis Club

**44** Abbeydale Park Sports Club

**45** Abbeydale Hall

**46** Brinkburn Grange

**47** Baslow Road meets Abbeydale Road South

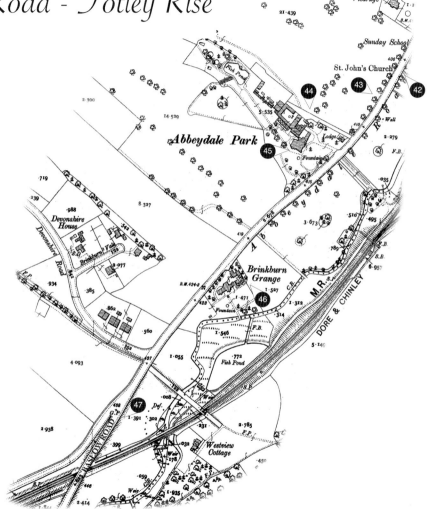

Map date 1905

St John's Church was built by John Roberts of Abbeydale Park. The Bishop of Lichfield consecrated the church in 1876. At that time it was in the diocese of Lichfield.

St John's Church Hall.

Note the mosaic nurse, clock and soldier above the entrance of the Church Hall. The hall was used as a Voluntary Aid Hospital during the First World War. In the year 1950 the hall was rented by the G.P.O for use as a sorting office. It was later bought by the G.P.O and is still a sorting office today.

Abbeydale Park Sports Club. The Park first opened for cricket in 1921, with the first pavilion being completed the following year. The first tenant was Sheffield Collegiate Cricket Club. The ground was in Derbyshire until the county boundary was redrawn in 1934, and Derbyshire County Cricket Club played two first-class matches there in 1946 and 1947.

With the closure of Bramall Lane to cricket, Yorkshire County Cricket Club began playing at the venue in 1974, and continued regular matches until 1996. In 2007, the club returned to the ground for some second team games.

In addition to cricket, football was also played at the Park, with Sheffield F.C., the oldest football club in the world, playing there from September 1921 until 1988. Argentina and Switzerland both trained at the ground during the 1966 World Cup.

Abbeydale Tennis Club was first established in 1929 and was one of the founder sports that formed Abbeydale Sports Club. In June 2009, thanks to £1m from the Lawn Tennis Association, Abbeydale Tennis Club upgraded its facilities with the aim of becoming one of the leading tennis centres in Yorkshire. The clubhouse was demolished to make way for a bigger building with improved changing rooms and better refreshment facilities. Disabled facilities are much improved too, and wheelchair tennis is now available for the first time in the club's 80-year history.

There are four indoor courts - two in a traditional structure plus two in the futuristic 'Airdome.' which can be easily seen from Abbeydale Road South.

Abbeydale Hall was built around 1860 and was the home of John Roberts - a Silversmith.

After John Roberts death, Ebenezer Hall, Mr Roberts apprentice and his wife Sarah moved into the hall.

The hall was later used by the Sheffield College for both day and evening classes. Part of the hall was also rented out for wedding receptions etc.

It has recently been converted into apartments and more new-build flats have been built in the grounds.

Ebenezer Hall and his wife Sarah.

Abbeydale Hall & Park. This photograph shows the hall fronting on to Abbeydale Road South. The fields behind rising up towards Dore.

Brinkburn Grange was an extensive manson situated close to Abbeydale Road South, opposite what is now Abbeydale Park Rise. It was built on land that was part of Bradway Mill in 1883 by Thomas B. Matthews. Mr Matthews was a director of Turton Brothers & Matthews, a Sheffield steel, file and spring makers. The mill dam was then used as an ornamental lake. The Grange was destroyed in 1938. The gate posts minus the stone balls on the top are the only reminder of what used to be there.

1961. Baslow Road meets Abbeydale Road South at Totley Rise, looking South from the railway bridge. Totley Methodist Church can be seen, over the bridge to the right.

# Other local titles available from Arc Publishing

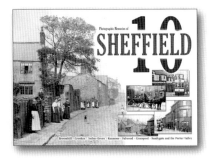

### Sheffield 10
Photographic memories of Broomhill, Crookes and many other suburbs of Sheffield 10. A fascinating look back in time which includes a journey through the Porter Valley.

£8.99

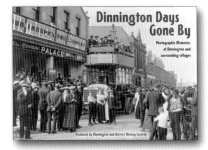

### Dinnington Days Gone By
A selection of photographs collected over many years by Dinnington & District History Society. The book shows the growth of Dinnington and the surrounding villages from their early beginnings as farming communities until the latter part of the 1900s.

£8.99

### Handsworth in days gone by
by Sandra Gillott
Sandra and the Handsworth Historical Society have put together this fascinating collection of photographs, many from the early 1900's. The local people, transport and buildings are all covered in this new book.

£8.99

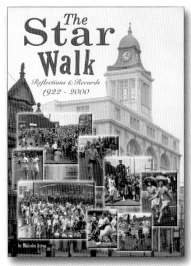

### The Star Walk (Reflections & Records 1922 - 2000)
This A4 size book with lots of photos, and information about the famous Star Walk that took place between 1922 and 2000. Many Sheffielders will have fond and nostalgic memories of this great sporting event. Malcolm Ayton author and walker in the races, has combined his recollection of the race with the records of runners over the years to give a fascinating enjoyable book.
£12.99

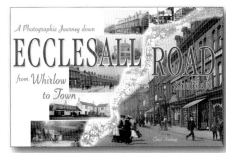

### ECCLESALL ROAD
### A photographic journey from Whirlow to Town
This is an informative enjoyable record of Ecclesall Road. Its rich diversity is well covered and brings back happy memories - travelling along one of Sheffield's finest roads. Certain stretches are still very recognizable but others near the city centre have changed dramatically.

Visit our website: www.sheffieldbooks.co.uk